CATCHING air

THE WILD WORLD OF SNOWBOARDING

BY GARY HUBBELL AND ROB GRACIE

Sports Illustrated KIDS FOR Books

CATCHING air

The awesome sport of snowboarding is growing by leaps and bounds.

INSIDE

INTRODUCTION

Do you want to have some fun? Try zooming down a snow-packed mountain with a snowboard strapped to your feet. Or fly off the snow-covered walls of a half-pipe (U-shaped ramp) and perform wild big-air tricks, flips, and spins. That's what snowboarders do. And it's fun.

The best boarders in the world like nothing better than to hit the slopes when they are covered with fine powder. They like to ride with friends and show off new tricks or race one another down a slalom course. There's one thing snowboarders *don't* like: rules. That's why they choose the sport. It doesn't have many rules.

Snowboarding leaves riders a lot of freedom and the opportunity to be creative. Do you want to become famous? Invent a new halfpipe trick that other snowboarders want to learn. Then admire how *differently* they do it.

In *Catching Air,* you will meet some of the best — and most unique — boarders in the world. You'll learn about the biggest boarding events and how it all got started. If you're itching to try the sport, there are tips for that, too.

So if you're ready to grab some serious air, just flip the page. And have fun! ∎

SNOWBOARDING

What sport combines the thrill of surfing with the speed of skiing and the creativity of skateboarding? The answer: snowboarding, the hottest sport around. Snowboarding has grown in just a few years. In 1993, 1.3 million boards were sold. That number rose to 2.5 million in 1997.

Snowboarding is really pretty simple: Take a board, strap it to your feet, and slide down the side of a mountain. It's totally cool!

HOW IT STARTED

Jake Burton helped to make snowboarding a hot sport.

SIMON BRUTY/SPORTS ILLUSTRATED

The first snowboard was actually a toy. In 1965, an American named Sherman Poppen invented the "Snurfer" for a sporting-goods company. He bolted two short skis together and made a surfboard for the snow. Riders stood on the board and held on to a rope that was attached to its tip.

In the 1970's, Jake Burton and Tom Sims helped to create the snowboards that are used today. Jake made the Snurfer board wider. He also added bindings that held a rider's feet in place. Soon, other people were making fiberglass boards.

In the mid-1970's, the first snowboards hit the stores.

HELMUT WAHL

Shaun Palmer (above) is super cool on a snowboard. He also has his own line of Palmer snowboards (far right).

THE BOARD

The average snowboard is six feet long and about nine inches wide. Most are made of fiberglass and wood with metal edges — just like skis. The boards have special bindings that snowboarding boots fit into.

HISTORY ❄

Todd Richards catches some air at the first Olympic snowboarding competition, in 1998.

WILLIAM R. SALLAZ

HOW IT'S DONE ❄

Organized snowboarding competition started in the early 1980's. Snowboarders now compete in world championships, at the Olympics, and at the X-Games (*see pages 24–28*).

Professional snowboarders compete in six events: slalom, parallel slalom, giant slalom, snowboardercross, super giant slalom, and halfpipe.

But "free riding," just riding down a mountain on your board is still at the heart of the sport. And many more people are doing it. In 1985, only 39 of the 600 ski areas in the U.S. allowed snowboarding. In 1997, only 12 *didn't*.

ROB GRACIE/PROMOTION

Snowboarders have a lot of moves. Some of them they do off the rim of the half-pipe, and some are done off jumps and bumps on the mountain. Basically, they do them wherever they can "catch air"! Most of these tricks are spectacular. And new ones are being invented all the time.

The names of the snowboard tricks usually give you some idea of what's happening in the trick: whether the board is being grabbed and where, how many spins are involved, and whether or not the rider flips upside down. ∎

Tail Grab Alley Oops

The boarder comes up off the jump, twists in the air 180 degrees (halfway around) while grabbing the tail of the board, and lands uphill from where she started. The grab helps prepare her for the spin.

Frontside 540

The boarder comes into the jump riding on the edge closest to his toes (called the toe-side edge). He jumps, twisting his arms and upper body in the opposite direction of where he's going. He grabs the front side of the board briefly. He lets go of the board and spins one-and-a-half times before landing.

Frontside Indy 720

The rider comes to the jump on his heel-side edge. He rotates his body to the heel-side edge as he grabs the board between his feet with the trailing hand. He does two full spins before landing.

Switch Backside 180

The boarder comes up to the lip of the jump with the tail of his board facing forward, which is called "switch." While in the air, he grabs the board and rotates half a turn so that he lands facing forward.

ROB GRACIE

Tail Grab McTwist

The rider comes up to the jump and does an upside-down spin (called an invert) while grabbing the board's tail. He also spins around 540 degrees before landing.

ILLUSTRATIONS BY JEAN WISENBAUGH

TERJE

COOL FACTS

BIRTH DATE:
October 11, 1974

BIRTHPLACE:
Aamot, Norway

HEIGHT: 5' 9"

WEIGHT:
150 pounds

HOMES:
Laguna Beach,
California,

and Oslo, Norway

**FAVORITE
SPORTS:**
Soccer, surfing,
and skating.

**FAVORITE
ATHLETES:**
Skateboarder
Tony Hawk and
soccer player
Diego Maradona

8

AAKONSEN

ARI MARCOPOULOS

Ask anyone in snowboarding *who* is the best rider in the world and the answer will always be the same: Terje Haakonsen *[TEAR-yay HAWK-on-sen].* What makes Terje so special? Big air! Terje soars an amazing *10* or *12 feet* into the air out of a halfpipe! He does dizzying spins and flips and always lands perfectly.

Terje grew up in Aamot, Norway. He skied downhill and cross-country. But at 13, he went snow-boarding with a friend. He loved it.

Terje won his first world halfpipe cham-pionship in 1992, when he was 17. Through 1998, he had won five European titles, three world championships, and three U.S. Open titles all in the halfpipe.

The only thing that stops Terje from winning is Terje: He doesn't like to enter competitions. He rides in only about 10 events a year. Terje didn't even go to the 1998 Olympics, when snowboarding was an official sport for the first time. Why? He didn't like all the rules!

"I just want to be around happy people in a good place," Terje says. "And riding a snowboard in lots of powder." ■

It's a bird! It's a plane! No! It's Terje shooting high into the air above the halfpipe.

COOL FACTS

BIRTH DATE:
November 26, 1972

BIRTHPLACE:
Steamboat Springs,
Colorado

HEIGHT: 5' 2"

WEIGHT:
110 pounds

HOME:
San Diego,
California

**FAVORITE
SPORTS:**
Mountain biking,
surfing, tennis and
golf

FAVORITE FOOD:
Smoothies

DID YOU KNOW?
Shannon travels
with her favorite
stuffed animal,
"Puppy."

SHANNON

ROB GRACIE

Shannon's stunning performance at the 1998 Olympics earned her the bronze medal.

DUNN

HIGH FLYERS

A good half-pipe rider is like an artist. She uses the snowboard to paint a series of beautiful jumps, spins, and tricks off the pipe. Maybe that's why Shannon Dunn is one of the best women halfpipe riders in the world. She is an artist.

When Shannon isn't riding her snowboard, she likes to sit down in front of her easel and paint watercolors. Each year, she designs the art for the top of her signature line of snowboards. Shannon is also illustrating a children's book written by a friend of hers.

When Shannon straps on her snowboard, her creativity makes her a star in the halfpipe. In 1997, she won the halfpipe events at both of the U.S. Snowboard Grand Prix championships and the Winter X-Games. Shannon also won a bronze medal at the 1998 Winter Olympic Games in Nagano, Japan. Shannon got into snowboarding because of her older brother, Sean. He taught her to snowboard at age 16. "I was hooked on snowboarding from that day on," says Shannon. She wasn't good at it at first. Shannon fell a lot and her body was very sore. But that didn't stop her.

"You can't really succeed without failing," Shannon says. "I fail more times than I succeed, but I believe you have to pick yourself up and keep going and never look back."

So far, Shannon has done just that. ∎

ROB GRACIE/LIFESTOCK

Mike Jacoby has always loved flying. He grew up near an airport in Idaho Falls, Idaho. Stunt pilots used to perform air shows there. Mike would ride his bike to the airport to watch the air shows.

Now, Mike does his his own flying — down the sides of snowy mountains. His blazing speed and ability to tackle the steepest mountains have earned him 11 giant slalom world cup titles since 1995.

Mike says snowboard racing is like flying. "Your board is working with the powder or snow and you can float through it," says Mike. "It's kind of the same thing with flying."

Mike started snowboarding at age 13. Mike and his friends would hike to the Idaho hills and board. He became a great free rider. But most of all, Mike loved going fast. When his family took vacations in Wyoming, he would grab his snowboard and ride the steepest mountains.

Mike is known for his tough training and dedication to fitness. He doesn't go to parties and hangs out by himself a lot. "I feel like I'm a hermit," he says.

Mike likes to mountain-bike and sky-surf. And he likes to fly *real* airplanes. Mike got his pilot's license in 1996 and hopes to be an airline pilot someday! ■

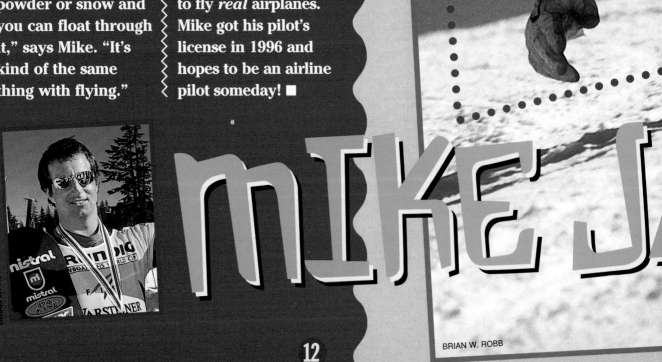

BRIAN W. ROBB

BRIAN W. ROBB

MIKE JA

At age 18, Mike won the slalom and giant slalom titles at the world amateur championship.

CODY

COOL FACTS

BIRTH DATE:
May 20, 1969

BIRTHPLACE:
Bellevue,
Washington

HEIGHT: 6' 1"

WEIGHT:
205 pounds

HOME:
Hood River, Oregon

FAVORITE SPORTS:
Skysurfing and kayaking

DID YOU KNOW?
Mike once rode his snowboard inside a volcano. He did it in 1994, for a movie called *Vertical Reality.*

COOL FACTS

BIRTH DATE: February 10, 1979

BIRTHPLACE: Bennington, Vermont

HEIGHT: 5' 9"

WEIGHT: 180 pounds

FAVORITE FOODS: Chinese, Mexican, and Italian

FAVORITE SPORTS TO PLAY: Mountain biking, moto-cross, football, baseball, and soccer

ROSS

POWERS

You're never too young to be a champion. Just ask Ross Powers. Ross became the world halfpipe champion at the tender age of 16!

When it comes to the halfpipe, Ross is the king. Some boarders are known for performing wild, original tricks off the pipe's walls. Others are known for grabbing a *lot* of air. Ross does both, in a big way!

It all started when Ross was 7. All he wanted for Christmas was a snowboard. His mother gave him one. Ross would practice at the Bromley ski resort, in Vermont, where his mom worked. Ross began entering snowboarding competitions when he was just 8.

In 1994, at age 15, Ross won the U.S. national halfpipe title. He beat out boarders who were much older than he was. At 16, he won his first world championship, in Lienz, Austria. At the 1998 Olympics, he earned a bronze medal in the first Olympics halfpipe competition.

What is Ross's secret to success? "I'm probably known for mixing it all together," Ross says.

His strategy seems to be working. The snowboarding world will be watching for Ross to mix it up in the years to come! ■

Up, up, and away! Ross soars to amazing heights performing in the halfpipe.

BRIAN W. ROBB (2)

Shaun's daredevil style has rocketed him to the top in snowboarding.

COOL FACTS

BIRTH DATE: November 14, 1968

BIRTHPLACE: South Lake Tahoe, California

HEIGHT: 5' 8"

WEIGHT: 175 pounds

HOME: South Lake Tahoe, California

FAVORITE SINGER: Frank Sinatra.

FAVORITE CAR: Cadillac. Shaun has three of them.

DID YOU KNOW? Shaun has his own series of Swatch watches with his name on them.

SHAUN PALMER

HIGH FLYERS

Shaun Palmer is the Dennis Rodman of snowboarding. He's flashy. He's fearless. His body is covered with weird tattoos and he wear lots of strange jewelry. He is also one of the best athletes in the world.

Shaun didn't win many friends when he first hit the snowboarding scene in 1985. He bragged a lot. He seemed to have a bad attitude. But Shaun had the drive and the talent to become a great boarder. He quickly proved himself.

Shaun is terrific in every snowboarding event — halfpipe, slalom, downhill, and snowboardercross. He has won world-class events in each of the four events. Shaun also won the boardercross title at the 1997 and 1998 X-Games.

But Shaun wasn't satisfied with being a super snowboarder. So in 1996, he began competing in mountain biking. Shaun even predicted he would become king of the mountain bike. He was right! He won the slalom title at the 1996 world mountain-bike championships.

Shaun had mastered two sports. Did he stop there? No way! In 1998, he made the finals of the LA Supercross, a national motocross event. He was now a top-level motorcycle racer.

"The best feeling in the world," Shaun says is "winning events."

The three-sport wonder should know.

PHOTOS COURTESY OF PALMER SNOWBOARDS (2)

17

MICHELE TAGGART

ROB GRACIE/LIFESTOCK

COOL FACTS

BIRTH DATE:
May 6, 1970

BIRTHPLACE:
Salem, Oregon

HEIGHT:
5' 6"

WEIGHT:
130 pounds

FAVORITE SPORTS:
Basketball, moto-cross, and surfing

FAVORITE PLACE TO RIDE: Alaska

DID YOU KNOW?
Michele went to college on a volley-ball scholarship.

When Michele Taggart fell in love with snow-boarding, she fell in love with *all* of it. And she got to be very good at all of it, too. She is a great half-pipe rider and awesome snowboard racer. In fact, Michele has won world titles in both halfpipe and giant slalom.

"It's hard doing both. I had to put in twice as much time as everyone else to keep on the same level," Michele says. All that training didn't leave her much time to just enjoy snowboarding.

After Michele won the International Snowboard Federation (ISF) giant slalom world champi-onship, in 1995, she decided to focus on the halfpipe. "I loved doing

Michele does it all! She has won world titles in both the half-pipe and giant slalom.

DAN HELMS

both events, but I wanted to free-ride a little more," she says.

The next year, Michele had a bad break. In December 1996, she fractured her leg. But by the end of the season, she was back competing! She placed fifth in the world halfpipe championships that year. Michele also competed at the 1998 Olympic Games.

Michele has always been a great athlete. When she was 17, her brother taught her to snowboard. Soon snowboarding was her life.

"I have the opportunity to travel and do something I want to do and get paid for it," says Michele. What's not to love in *that*?

SONDRA

Before Sondra Van Ert ever even got on a snowboard, she had already retired from World Cup competition. World Cup *skiing* competition, that is!

Sondra grew up in Bountiful, Utah. She started skiing when she was 3 years old. In 1984, she became a downhill racer on the U.S. Ski Team.

After two years on the World Cup skiing circuit, Sondra quit. She had injured her knee and was burned out. She decided to go to college.

Then, one day in 1990, she saw a bunch of kids in Sun Valley, Idaho, ripping by on their snowboards. Soon Sondra was boarding herself. "I did a fun race, and it went well," Sondra says. "Pretty soon, I was back in the World Cup, ten years after being done with it."

In 1997, Sondra won the world giant slalom snowboarding championship. In 1998, at age 33, Sondra was hoping to win the gold medal at the Winter Olympics, in Nagano, Japan. But she fell during her first run on the tricky course. After a good second run, she finished in 12th place.

Did Sondra think about retiring? No way! After the Games, she started training for the next season. She even talks about competing at the 2002 Olympics!

"I plan to race as long as I can stay competitive," Sondra says.

Besides, she already knows what retirement is like! ∎

COOL FACTS

BIRTH DATE:
March 9, 1964

BIRTHPLACE:
Des Moines, Iowa

HEIGHT:
5' 9"

WEIGHT:
140 pounds

HOME:
Ketchum, Idaho

FAVORITE ANIMAL: Monkey. She collects stuffed-animal monkeys.

FAVORITE SPORTS:
Mountain biking, backpacking, skiing, mountain boarding (an off-road skateboard with big wheels)

DID YOU KNOW?:
Sondra works in avalanche control at the Sun Valley (Idaho) ski area. Her dog, Avy, used to be an avalanche rescue dog.

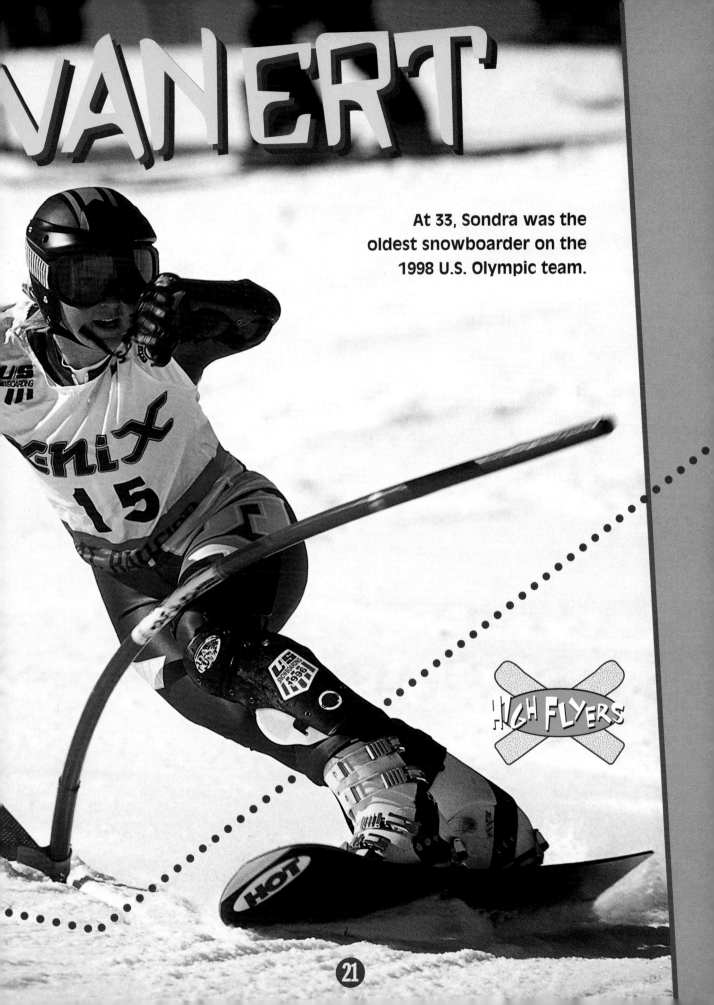

VANERT

At 33, Sondra was the oldest snowboarder on the 1998 U.S. Olympic team.

HIGH FLYERS

KARINE RUBY

Karine's nerves of steel helped her capture the gold medal at the 1998 Winter Olympics.

Many athletes try to keep themselves calm before a big competition. Not Karine Ruby. The giant-slalom racer actually works at getting herself nervous before a race.

"I always perform better when I'm tense," says Karine, "so I try to stress myself out a bit before a competition." The ploy seems to be working. The 20-year-old French woman has won two world championships and an Olympic gold.

When Karine won six World Cup giant-slalom snowboard races in 1998, everyone expected her to win a gold medal at the Olympics. But the course in Nagano, Japan, was so tricky, even some of the best boarders crashed. Not Karine. She mastered the course and took home the gold.

Karine grew up in Chamonix *[sha-muh-NEE]*, France. Her parents started snowboarding when Karine was 9. She joined them at age 10.

From the beginning, Karine liked to ride with the boys. She says that helped her become mentally tough.

"My advantage is that I know no fear," Karine says. "I always trained with boys and learned from them how to overcome fear." ∎

COOL FACTS

BIRTH DATE:
January 4, 1978

BIRTHPLACE:
Bonneville, France

HEIGHT: 5' 5"

WEIGHT:
132 pounds

FAVORITE SPORTS:
Rock climbing and paragliding

BIGGEST SPORTS THRILL:
"The Olympics — the moment when I crossed the finish line and realized what had happened."

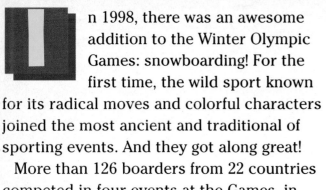

In 1998, there was an awesome addition to the Winter Olympic Games: snowboarding! For the first time, the wild sport known for its radical moves and colorful characters joined the most ancient and traditional of sporting events. And they got along great!

More than 126 boarders from 22 countries competed in four events at the Games, in Nagano, Japan.

Only giant slalom and halfpipe events were held at the Nagano Games. There were separate competitions for men and women.

In the giant slalom, boarders race, one at a time, down a half-mile-long course. They carve fast turns between about 45 gates as they try to get to the bottom. Each racer gets two tries. The speediest racer wins.

In halfpipe, boarders zip up and down the sides of a U-shaped ramp while performing tricks off the rim.

Snowboarding made such a big splash at the Olympics, fans can't wait for the 2002 Games. ◘■

MIKE HEWITT/ALLSPORT

ON THE EDGE

EVENTS

MEN'S
Giant Slalom
Halfpipe
WOMEN'S
Giant Slalom
Halfpipe

MARK GALLUP

Karine Ruby (center) rode away with the gold in women's giant slalom at Nagano.

24

OLYMPICS

Michele Taggart of the U.S. put a new spin on her halfpipe performance.

Veli Kestenholz placed third when snowboarding made its Olympic debut.

X-GAMES

105

Since they started
in 1995, the
X-Games have
really taken off!

EVENTS
**MEN'S and
WOMEN'S**
Halfpipe
Snowboardercross
Slopestyle
Big Air

Snowboarding in July? Sounds crazy, but it's true! You will find it only at the X-Games. In 1995, the cable sports channel ESPN launched the X-Games. They feature radical sports such as snowboarding, kite-skiing, in-line skating, skateboarding, and mountain biking. They are held every year.

The X-Games became so popular, ESPN added the Winter X-Games in 1997. But you can still see snowboarding at the Summer X-Games. For the 1998 X-Games, snow was flown into sunny San Diego, California, in July!

Four boarding events are held at the X-Games: big air, halfpipe, snowboardercross, and slopestyle.

Big air is held on a big snow jump instead of a halfpipe. One by one, boarders fly off the jump. They are judged on their jump, tricks, and landing.

In snowboardercross, racers try to be the first to get down a mountain full of bumps and jumps. Six boarders start each heat together. Two or three of the fastest riders move on to the next round. Whoever wins the final race gets the prize.

The slopestyle course has more difficult jumps and bumps than snowboardercross. Riders race against the clock and do tricks off the jumps. ■

NATHAN BILOW/ALLSPORT

ROB GRACIE

NATHAN BILOW/ALLSPORT

Steve Adkins powered himself to higher heights in 1998.

Jamil Kahn's high-flying heroics awed fans at the 1998 Winter X-Games.

At the 1996 Worlds, Germany's Peter Bauer blazed down this tricky slalom course.

EVENTS

MEN'S and WOMEN'S
Giant Slalom
Slalom
Halfpipe
Parallel Slalom
Boardercross

ROB GRACIE

Away he goes! This boarder jumped at the chance to win a world title.

MIKE COOPER/ALLSPORT

Boarders save some of their best moves for the world championships.

Every two years, the best boarders in the world compete in the world championships, held by the International Ski Federation (FIS). The winner of each event earns the title of world champion, along with lots of cash.

Boarders compete in five events at the world championships: giant slalom, slalom, halfpipe, parallel slalom, and boardercross. There are separate events for men and women.

Parallel slalom is an exciting event that is not held at the Olympics or X-Games. Two courses are side-by-side. Boarders travel down the two courses at the same time, making quick, tight, turns. The boarder gets two tries and the one with the fastest combined time on both runs wins.

The FIS also holds a junior world championship for boarders under 18. Juniors compete in giant slalom and halfpipe. ■

THE BASICS

GETTING STARTED

Are you ready to hit the slopes? Here's what you need to know.

1 Rent boots and a board. (Don't buy anything until you know what you're doing.) You can rent your stuff at a ski store or at the ski area.

2 Sign up for lessons at a ski area. You can get a package that includes renting a board and boots, a group lesson, and a lift ticket for $70 to $100 per day.

3 Get ready to fall a lot! That's part of the fun.

For More Information write to:
U.S. Snowboarding,
Box 100
Park City, Utah 84060

EQUIPMENT

GOGGLES

BAGGY WATER-PROOF PANTS

TOE-SIDE EDGE

TAIL

NOSE

HEEL-SIDE EDGE

EDGES

Snowboards are designed to be ridden on their edges. You rarely slide on the flat bot-

tom of the board. Try to turn from one edge to the other, digging the uphill edge into the snow. The edge beneath your toes is the toe edge, and the edge beneath your heels is the heel edge.

STANCE

Your first snowboarding trick will be figuring out which foot goes forward on your board. Ask for help at a ski shop. Most people ride "regular," with their left foot forward. *Goofy* is an old surfing term for people who place their right foot forward.

THE BOARDS

You need a snowboard, boots, and bindings. A board with bindings costs $350 to $400. Boots cost about $150 to $225.

There are three types of boards:

FREERIDE

Most snowboarders use this type of board. It is great for flying off bumps and for going on or off the groomed trails. Both the front and the back of the freeride board curve up. You can turn it around and ride it with either foot forward.

ALPINE

This board is narrower and stiffer than a freeride board. It makes you go very fast and is great for carving turns.

FREESTYLE

This type is best for doing tricks in a halfpipe. It is wider and shorter than a freeride or an alpine board.

After you choose a type of board, ask the people at the ski shop to help you select the right size board. Your boots and bindings also should match the type of riding you do.

Snowboarders used to wear fat, baggy pants and baggy flannel shirts. Now they wear clothing that is tighter but baggy enough for doing radical tricks. The best pants and tops are warm and weatherproof. You'll also want warm socks, waterproof gloves, sunglasses, and a hat.

THE BASICS

TOE-SIDE TURN

Keep your weight forward slightly and bend your knees. Gently twist your upper body toward your toe-side edge and look in the direction you want to turn. Lean forward to press the board's toe-side edge into the snow. Keep your hands in front of your body at waist level.

HEEL-SIDE TURN

Follow the instructions for the toe-side turn. This time, turn your upper body toward your heel-side edge and lift your toes to press your heel-side edge into the snow. After you learn both turns, practice "linking" turns. Simply turn back and forth all the way down the mountain.

!SUPER TIP!

LINGO

Toe Edge: The edge of the board by your toes

Heel Edge: The edge of the board by your heels

Regular: A snowboard stance with the left foot forward

Goofy: A snowboard stance with the right foot forward

Fakie: Riding goofy, if you normally ride regular, or regular if you normally ride goofy

Catching Air: Jumping or flying off a bump or cliff

Halfpipe: A snow-covered, U-shaped section of a hill where snowboarders do tricks

Bonk: Bouncing off a tree stump or another object with your board

Skating: Using your rear foot to push yourself over flat ground

---

!SUPER TIP!

Take off
Bend
Grab

Stand

INDY AIR

After you learn to "catch air" off a bump or jump, you can start adding mid-air tricks. One of the simplest air tricks is the Indy Air. As soon as you launch off the jump, bend your knees and bring the board up toward your rear end. At the same time, bend at the waist, reach down with your back hand, and grab the toe edge of the board between your feet. Hold on to the board as long as you want. Keep your front arm stretched to the side, for balance. Keep your weight centered over the board and your eyes focused on your landing spot. As you drop to the ground, let go of the board and stand up. Keep your knees bent for a soft landing.

Land